My Favourite Recipes

First printed 2011
Eaglemoss Publications Group, 1st Floor, Beaumont House,
Kensington Village, Avonmore Road,
London W14 8TS

ISSN 2043-0892
123456789

Reproduction by F E Burmans, UK.
Printed in the EU by Imprimerie Pollina.

My Favourite Recipes
Easy Eggs & Cheese
Front cover: David Munns/Prima/NMC (t), David Munns/Prima/NMC (bl), William Shaw/Prima/NMC (br), 8 Jon Whittaker/Prima/NMC, 9 Tim Winter/Prima/NMC (t), Iain Bagwell/Prima/NMC (bl), Prima/NMC (bc), Jon Whittaker/Prima/NMC (br), 10 Liz Parsons/Prima/NMC, 11 EM/Ken Field, 12 David Munns/Prima/NMC, 13 Sam Stowell/Prima/NMC (t), Jon Whittaker/Prima/NMC (b), 14 Jon Whittaker/Prima/NMC, 16 Jon Whittaker/Prima/NMC, 18 David Munns/Prima/NMC, 18 Prima/NMC, 20 Poisson D'avril/PhotoCuisine, 22 William Shaw/Prima/NMC, 24 Jon Whittaker/Prima/NMC, 26 Descordes/PhotoCuisine, 28 Tim Winter/Prima/NMC, 30 William Shaw/Prima/NMC, 32 Jon Whittaker/Prima/NMC, 34 David Munns/Prima/NMC, 36 David Munns/Prima/NMC, 38 Ryman/PhotoCuisine, 40 Jon Whittaker/Prima/NMC, 42 Jon Whittaker/Prima/NMC, 44 Marie Louise Avery/Prima/NMC, 46 Jon Whittaker/Prima/NMC, 48 Sean Myers/Prima/NMC, 50 EM/Jon Asprey, 52 Riou/PhotoCuisine, 54 Iain Bagwell/Prima/NMC, 56 Jon Whittaker/Prima/NMC, 58 EM/Thomas Odulate, 58 Juliet Piddington/Prima/NMC, 59 Roulier/Turiot/PhotoCuisine, 60 Juliet Piddington/Prima/NMC, 62 Jon Whittaker/Prima/NMC, 64 Jon Whittaker/Prima/NMC, 66 Jon Whittaker/Prima/NMC, 68 Jon Whittaker/Prima/NMC, 70 Jon Whittaker/Prima/NMC, 72 Tim Winter/Prima/NMC, 74 Jon Whittaker/Prima/NMC, 76 Pete Cassidy/Prima/NMC, 78 EM/Karl Adamson, 80 Geoff Fenney/Prima/NMC, 82 Tim Winter/Prima/NMC, 84 Phillip Webb/Prima/NMC, 86 Sirois/PhotoCuisine, 88 EM/Martin Brigdale, 90 Tim Winter/Prima/NMC, 92 EM/Amanda Heywood.

EM = Eaglemoss Publications Group
NMC = The National Magazine Company

My Favourite Recipes

Easy Eggs & Cheese

My Favourite Recipes

The most humble ingredients are often the most versatile, and egg and cheese are no exception. Most of us keep a box of eggs and a block or two of cheese in the house, but you may not realise just how many tempting dishes you can rustle up from these storecupboard favourites.

We've collected a great selection of family favourites, like macaroni cheese, toasties, quiches and omelettes, plus some new ideas and smarter recipes, perfect for relaxed entertaining. Try your hand at a light and fluffy soufflé (it's easier than you think) or create a classic baked cheesecake or custard tart.

With so many varieties of cheese now readily available, you can vary the flavour and create all kinds of great dishes. Try griddled halloumi cheese with Mediterranean vegetables or deep-fry some creamy Camembert in golden breadcrumbs – irresistible!

So get cracking, and try some of these superb suppers and snacks.

Happy cooking!

Becky Davis

Editor

My Favourite Recipes

Contents

Camembert Croquettes

Four Cheese Focaccia

American Cheesecake

Key to recipe symbols

Super Quick
Ready in under 15 minutes.

Quick
Ready in 30 minutes or less.

Make it at the Weekend
This dish needs a little more attention so make it when you have extra time to spare.

✓ *Easy*
Simple to prepare for most cooks.

✓✓ *Extra Easy*
Simple to prepare, even for an inexperienced cook.

Freeze it
This recipe can be frozen.

Spicy
This recipe has a bit of a kick!

N *Contains Nuts*
This recipe contains nuts.

V *Vegetarian*
This recipe is suitable for vegetarians.

Excellent Eggs

Baked, boiled, scrambled, fried, in an omelette, whisked into a batter or used for baking, eggs must be one of the most versatile ingredients around.

With a box of eggs in the house you'll never be short of a quick and easy meal. They can be cooked in so many ways, from the humble boiled egg to fancy frittatas, pancakes and fritters, that you need never be stuck for ideas to please all the family.

ONE-PAN WONDERS

An omelette is ideal as a quick supper or lunch. You can add your choice of flavourings to suit what you have in the fridge or cupboard and simply serve on its own, with bread or salad. Go for classic fillings like cheese, ham, mushrooms or tomatoes, or try something more exotic such as stir-fried vegetables, roasted peppers from a jar or canned artichokes. A frittata or tortilla is a thicker, set version of an omelette and can include things like fried sliced potatoes and onions, cooked spaghetti and red or green pesto, or a selection of cooked meat and veg.

Breakfast Ideas

- **You can't beat a simple boiled egg for breakfast. Place the eggs in a pan of boiling water for 4 minutes, then drain. Serve with toast soldiers spread with butter or yeast extract.**
- **Poached eggs are another great idea for a healthy breakfast. Bring a large pan of water to the boil. Crack the eggs into cups. Swirl the water and slide in the eggs. Cook gently for 3–4 minutes until just set. Serve on toasted muffins or steamed spinach.**
- **Creamy scrambled eggs are a quick and easy breakfast favourite. See our three tasty variations (right) or serve plain or with strips of smoked salmon.**
- **For French toast, beat eggs with a little milk and season. Dip in slices of bread and fry in butter until golden.**

Potato & Chive Pancake

This is a great budget supper using a handful of basic ingredients. Serve with sausage, bacon or tomatoes instead of the peppers.

3 medium potatoes, unpeeled
1 pack fresh chives, finely chopped
2 eggs, beaten and seasoned
1–2 tablespoons plain flour
1 tablespoon olive oil
Knob of butter
Roasted or fried peppers, to serve

● Cook the unpeeled potatoes in a pan of boiling water until soft. Drain and cool. ● Peel and grate the cold potatoes. Mix with the chives, eggs and flour. ● Heat the oil and butter in a pan and tip in the potato mix. Flatten out to fill the pan. ● Cook for 5 minutes until set underneath. ● Turn onto a plate and return to pan to cook the other side. Serve with peppers.

FLIPPING GREAT!

Pancakes are always popular and can be sweet or savoury. See our basic recipe on page 18 and team with your favourite fillings. Try sugar and lemon or bananas and toffee sauce for a sweet treat, or fill with ham and cheese, chicken in white sauce, ratatouille or spinach and ricotta. For fritters, add a teaspoon of baking powder and reduce the milk by half to make a thicker batter. Add canned sweetcorn or grated courgettes and fry spoonfuls until golden and set.

3 Ways with... Scrambled Eggs

Great for breakfast, lunch or supper, scrambled eggs are the ultimate quick meal. Try these new flavour ideas.

1 *Beat the eggs with a dash of Thai fish sauce, a pinch of sugar, chopped red chilli and crushed garlic. Cook briefly then add cooked peeled prawns and fresh coriander. Cook to your liking.*

2 *Fry chopped onion and red pepper in oil until soft. Add chopped tomatoes and cook until soft and juices have evaporated. Add eggs and stir until just set. Garnish with chopped parsley.*

3 *Fry chopped spring onions and tomatoes in oil until soft. Add pinch of cumin then the eggs and fresh parsley. Cook until just set but still creamy, then sprinkle with cayenne or paprika.*

Sensational Soufflés

Light, tasty and so impressive – there's nothing quite like a savoury soufflé to add the wow factor to your dinner table, and it's easier than you think to make.

The secret to successful soufflés is to follow a few basic rules – make sure you weigh the ingredients accurately, whisk the eggs whites to the right stiff peak stage and set the oven to the right temperature. After that you'll find soufflés make a great standby dish for entertaining friends and family.

EGG TIPS

When making a soufflé, make sure the eggs are at room temperature before you start. If you keep your eggs in the fridge (which isn't necessary) take them out at least an hour before using. Egg whites whisk more quickly and to a greater volume if they are not too cold.

FULL OF FLAVOUR

The basic cheese soufflé tastes great but you can add almost any ingredient you like for extra flavour (see our tasty ideas (below right)). Bulky ingredients should be minced, diced or puréed so they are not too heavy to be supported by the mixture. Heavy ingredients could stop the soufflé rising effectively.

Twice-baked Soufflés

These are baked once until risen then baked again before serving – perfect prepare ahead dishes for entertaining.

- **Melt the butter as in the main recipe then add a finely sliced leek and fry until soft. Add the flour and milk as directed to make the sauce. Stir in 50g (2oz) grated Gruyère and 2 egg yolks.**
- **Whisk 2 egg whites until stiff then fold in the leek mixture. Spoon into 4 buttered ramekins and bake for 15 minutes until risen. Cool and keep chilled.**
- **To reheat, increase oven to 200°C/400°F/Gas 6. Turn out the soufflés into a buttered ovenproof dish. Top each one with some grated Parmesan and a spoonful of single cream. Bake again for 10 minutes until risen and golden.**

SERVING TIPS

Your soufflé should really be the star of the show so keep accompaniments simple – a green salad and some crusty bread is all you need. The soufflé needs to be served straight from the oven before it collapses.

Different Flavours

- **Add cooked, mashed broccoli or cauliflower to the soufflé.**
- **Cooked spinach, steamed asparagus or sautéed mushrooms work well.**
- **Add smoked haddock flakes, canned tuna or crab for a fishy dish.**
- **Slivers of cooked ham, bacon or chicken mixed with fresh herbs make a tasty addition.**
- **Vary the cheese used – try Stilton, Gruyère, Lancashire or Roquefort.**

Quicker Than You Think...

Classic Cheese Soufflé

Impress your family and friends with a towering golden soufflé. It's easier than you think with our helpful step-by-step guide.

Serves 4

Preparation 20 mins
Cooking 30 mins
276 Kcals & 20.5g fat

1 tablespoon grated Parmesan
25g (1oz) butter
2 tablespoons plain flour
2 teaspoons English mustard powder
Salt and freshly ground black pepper
200ml (7fl oz) milk
4 large eggs, separated, plus 1 white
75g (3oz) mature Cheddar, finely grated

1 Preheat oven to 190°C/375°F/Gas 5. Sprinkle Parmesan into 1.4 ltr (2½pt) soufflé dish, tilting to coat sides. Chill. Melt the butter in a pan and stir in the flour and mustard. Season. Cook for 2 minutes, stirring.

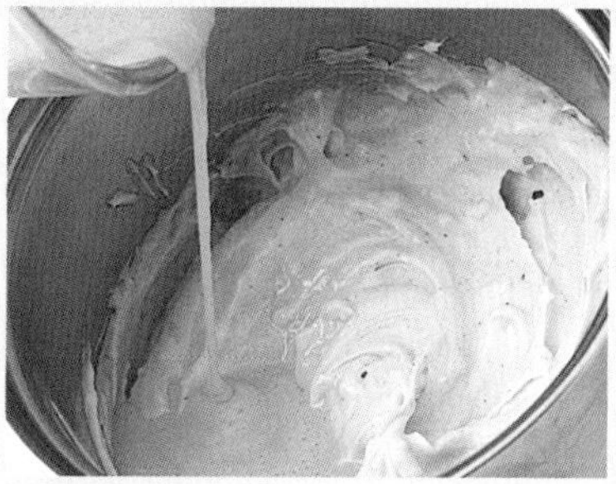

2 Gradually stir in the milk and cook, stirring until boiled and thickened. Beat in the egg yolks, one at a time. Stir in the Cheddar, reserving 1 tablespoon.

3 Whisk the egg whites until stiff peaks form. Fold in the sauce until just combined. Pour into dish, and run a knife around the edge. Sprinkle with cheese. Bake on a tray for 30 minutes until just firm.

TOP TIPS

- **Running a knife around the edge of the soufflé mixture before baking stops it sticking and helps it to rise evenly.**
- **The cooking times here give a light texture with a hint of creaminess in the middle. For a firmer set, bake at 180°C/350°F/Gas 4 for 35 minutes or increase the oven to 200°C/400°F/Gas 6 and bake for 25 minutes for a gooey centre.**
- **Don't be tempted to look into the oven too early – allow at least 20 minutes before opening the door. A sudden temperature drop can mean disaster!**

Say Cheese!

From the classic cheese on toast to pizzas, fondues, pasta dishes, bakes, soufflés and omelettes, cheese is the perfect ingredient for a supper or snack.

With so many different varieties to choose from, cheese is a really versatile and tasty ingredient. Hard cheeses like Cheddar and Gruyère are perfect for grating or slicing, while soft cheeses like ricotta and mascarpone can be stirred into all kinds of dishes. Plus there are all the different varieties in between like salty Greek feta (great for crumbling into salads and pasta dishes), halloumi (ideal grilled or griddled), tangy goat's cheese (grill, crumble or melt into sauces) and soft, mild mozzarella (perfect for pizzas and paninis).

TOP TOASTIES

Cheese on toast is a classic quick supper or after-school treat but don't just stick to the basic recipe, try something new. Spread the bread with wholegrain mustard, pesto, tomato sauce or chutney for extra

471 Kcals and 26g fat per portion (serves 4)

Panini Pizzas

2 panini rolls
1 garlic clove, peeled and cut in half
2 tablespoons olive oil
½ x 280g jar chargrilled artichokes in oil, drained and halved
8–10 pieces sun-dried tomato, drained and sliced
2 x 125g balls mozzarella, drained and sliced
Freshly ground black pepper
Handful fresh basil leaves

● Preheat the oven to 170°C/325°F/Gas 3. ● Split the paninis in half and rub the cut sides with the halved garlic clove. ● Drizzle with olive oil. Place on a baking tray. ● Arrange the artichokes, tomatoes and mozzarella on top and finish with a grinding of black pepper. ● Bake for 10–15 minutes until the cheese is melted and oozing. ● Serve warm scattered with fresh basil leaves.

336 Kcals and 18.8g fat per portion (serves 4)

Bruschetta with Goat's Cheese

4 thick slices crusty bread
1 garlic clove, peeled and cut in half
2 tablespoons olive oil
4 tomatoes, deseeded and chopped
1 teaspoon fresh thyme leaves
Salt and freshly ground black pepper
4 thick slices firm goat's cheese

● Preheat the grill to high. Toast the bread until golden on both sides. ● Rub the toast with the halved garlic clove, then drizzle with half the olive oil and place on a baking tray. ● Mix together the tomatoes, thyme leaves, remaining oil and seasoning. ● Spoon onto the toasts and top each one with a slice of goat's cheese. ● Grill until the cheese is melted and oozing. ● Season with plenty of black pepper and serve warm.

flavour. Add some sliced tomatoes, ham, canned tuna, roasted peppers or bacon underneath the cheese. Vary the bread too – muffins, bagels, ciabatta, paninis and sourdough bread all work well.

SUPER SNACKS

For an alternative toastie, sprinkle a soft flour or corn tortilla with grated cheese (and any other ingredients you like), top with a second tortilla and fry in a lightly oiled pan, turning halfway through, until golden and the cheese is starting to melt. Or try the French favourite, croque monsieur. Top slices of toasted crusty bread with ruffles of lean ham. Mix grated cheese with a little cream and Dijon mustard and spread over the ham. Grill until golden and bubbling.

390 Kcals and 5g fat per portion (serves 4)

Courgette & Cottage Cheese Pasta

350g (12oz) short pasta shapes
Salt and freshly ground black pepper
100g (3½oz) peas
1 large courgette
250g (9oz) cottage cheese
2 tablespoons chopped fresh mint
2 tablespoons lemon juice
Handful torn fresh basil leaves

● Cook the pasta in a pan of boiling salted water according to the pack instructions until just tender. Add the peas for the last few minutes cooking time. ● Drain in a colander then cool under cold running water. Drain again. ● Coarsely grate the courgette into a large bowl. Add the cottage cheese and mint and mix well. Season with salt and freshly ground black pepper. ● Add the pasta and peas and stir to combine. ● Squeeze over the lemon juice and serve sprinkled with fresh basil. ● This can be covered and chilled overnight until ready to eat.

Quick · Extra Easy · Vegetarian

Tomato & Herb Frittata

Preparation time 15 minutes ● Cooking time 15 minutes

6 tomatoes, roughly chopped

Olive oil, for drizzling

Salt and freshly ground black pepper

Bunch fresh mixed herbs (chives, basil and parsley work well), roughly chopped

6 eggs, lightly whisked

- **1** Place the tomatoes in a large bowl and drizzle with olive oil. Season with salt and black pepper, then stir in the herbs. (Leave to stand for 10 minutes if you have time for the flavours to develop.)
- **2** Preheat the grill to high. Heat a medium-sized non-stick frying pan over a low heat. Add the tomatoes and some of the oil and stir into an even layer, then cook for 1 minute. Season the eggs and pour into the pan to cover the tomatoes. Cook for 10–12 minutes until the base is cooked.
- **3** Pop the frying pan under the hot grill until the top is set and lightly golden. Slip a palette knife under the frittata, transfer to a plate and serve.

Calories per portion 206 Kcal ● Fat per portion 16g ● Serves 4

Serve with...

Serve this tasty dish with a simple green salad drizzled with olive oil.

Why not try...

If your frying pan handle isn't heatproof, wrap it in foil before grilling. Take care when handling as it will get very hot – always use oven gloves.

✓ *Easy* *Spicy* Ⓥ *Vegetarian*

Boiled Eggs & Lentil Dahl

Preparation time 15 minutes ● Cooking time 45 minutes

4 eggs

1 tablespoon olive oil

1 large onion, finely chopped

1 red and 1 green chilli, deseeded and finely chopped

1½ teaspoons coriander seeds, lightly crushed

2 garlic cloves, finely chopped

¼ teaspoon ground cumin

3 bay leaves

5cm (2in) piece fresh ginger, peeled and finely chopped

250g (9oz) red lentils, washed

Zest of 1 lemon

½ teaspoon ground cinnamon

750ml (1¼pts) hot vegetable stock

3 tomatoes, finely chopped

Small bunch fresh coriander, roughly chopped

● **1** Place the eggs in a pan of water and bring to the boil. Simmer for 6–8 minutes until hard-boiled. Drain and leave to cool in cold water.

● **2** Heat the oil in a frying pan and add the onion, chillies, coriander seeds, garlic, cumin, bay leaves and ginger. Cook over a medium heat for 5 minutes until the onion has softened.

● **3** Add the lentils, lemon zest and cinnamon, then pour over the stock. Simmer, uncovered, for 25–30 minutes, stirring occasionally, until the lentils are soft. Stir in the tomatoes and heat through before adding the coriander. Peel and halve the eggs and add to the dahl.

Calories per portion 360 Kcal ● Fat per portion 3g ● Serves 4

Serve with...

Serve this aromatic dish with warm chapatis or naan breads.

✓ *Easy* Ⓥ *Vegetarian*

Mushroom Pancake Stack

Preparation time 15 minutes ● Cooking time 30 minutes

2 tablespoons olive oil

250g pack mushrooms, thinly sliced

200ml carton crème fraîche

Handful chopped fresh parsley, plus extra to garnish

Splash of lemon juice

For the pancakes

125g (4oz) plain flour

Salt and freshly ground black pepper

1 large egg

300ml (½pt) milk

Oil or melted butter, for frying

● **Step 1** Sift the flour and a pinch of salt into a bowl. Make a well in the centre and add the egg and half the milk. Whisk together, gradually blending in the flour, to make a smooth batter. Stir in the remaining milk.

● **Step 2** Heat a little oil or butter in a medium frying pan, then tip the excess into a bowl. Pour in some batter, tilting the pan so the base is thinly coated. Cook over a medium heat for 30–60 seconds until golden underneath.

● **Step 3** Flip over the pancake with a palette knife, and cook the other side until golden brown. Slide the pancake onto a plate, and cook the remaining batter in the same way to make 6 pancakes. Layer between sheets of greaseproof paper and keep warm.

● **4** Heat the olive oil in a frying pan and cook the mushrooms until tender. Stir in the crème fraîche and parsley. Season and add a squeeze of lemon juice. Bubble gently for 5 minutes until thickened. Layer the pancakes with the mushroom mixture and sprinkle with a little more parsley.

Calories per portion 318 Kcal ● Fat per portion 24.3g ● Serves 6

Step 1 *Add the egg and half the milk to the flour and whisk thoroughly to form a smooth lump-free batter.*

Step 2 *Pour a little batter into the hot pan and tilt gently to cover the base evenly. Cook until golden underneath.*

Step 3 *Flip over the pancake with a palette knife and cook the other side until golden. Transfer to a plate.*

Make it at the Weekend

Quiche Lorraine

Preparation time 20 minutes plus chilling ● Cooking time 45 minutes

225g (8oz) plain flour

Salt and freshly ground black pepper

50g (2oz) butter, diced

50g (2oz) lard, diced

125g (4oz) back bacon, chopped

125g (4oz) Gruyère, thinly sliced

3 eggs, beaten

150ml (¼pt) single cream

● **1** Sift the flour and a pinch of salt into a bowl. Rub in the butter and lard with your fingertips until the mixture resembles breadcrumbs. Add enough chilled water to bind to a dough. Roll into a ball, wrap in cling film and chill in the fridge for 20 minutes.

● **2** Preheat the oven to 200°C/400°F/Gas 6. Roll out the pastry on a floured surface and use to line a small rectangular or 20.5cm (8in) round tin.

● **3** Line the pastry with foil or greaseproof paper and weight down with baking beans. Bake for 10 minutes. Remove the beans and foil and return to the oven for a further 5 minutes until set and pale golden.

● **4** Sprinkle the bacon over the pastry base, then scatter over the cheese. Beat together the eggs, cream and seasoning and pour into the pastry case. Bake for 30 minutes until set and golden brown.

Calories per portion 731 Kcal ● Fat per portion 51.1g ● Serves 4

Serve with...

Serve the quiche hot or cold, garnished with parsley and served with salad.

Why not try...

To save time, use ready-made shortcrust pastry instead of making your own.

Baked Scotch Eggs

Preparation time 20 minutes ● Cooking time 30 minutes

6 eggs

10 sausages, skinned

Plain flour, to dust

1 egg, beaten

125g (4oz) fresh fine breadcrumbs, lightly toasted

- **1** Preheat the oven to 180°C/350°F/Gas 4. Place the eggs in a pan of water and bring to the boil. Simmer for 4–6 minutes until cooked to your liking. Drain, cool under cold running water and peel off the shells.
- **2** Mix the sausagemeat in a bowl. Divide into 6 and flatten with your hand. Dust each egg in a little flour then wrap the sausage meat around, moulding it so there are no gaps. It should be about 5mm (¼in) thick.
- **3** Place a little more flour on a shallow plate, the beaten egg in a shallow bowl and the breadcrumbs on a plate. Roll each egg in flour, then beaten egg and finally in breadcrumbs until totally covered.
- **4** Place the eggs on a baking sheet or roasting tin and bake for about 15–20 minutes until golden and the sausage meat is cooked. Serve hot or cold.

Calories per portion 433 Kcal ● Fat per portion 10g ● Serves 6

Serve with...

Serve the eggs hot or cold with a selection of salads and chutney.

Why not try...

Traditionally Scotch eggs are deep-fried. Heat about 6cm (2½in) oil in a deep pan and fry the coated eggs for 3–4 minutes, turning occasionally.

✓ *Easy* *Spicy* Ⓥ *Vegetarian*

Mexican Baked Eggs

Preparation time 10 minutes ● Cooking time 30 minutes

1 tablespoon olive oil, plus 2 teaspoons for brushing
1 onion, chopped
650g (1lb 7oz) mixed peppers (about 4), deseeded and chopped
Large pinch dried chilli flakes
450g (1lb) mixed fresh tomatoes, large ones chopped
1 teaspoon smoked or sweet paprika
400g can black beans, rinsed and drained
Salt and freshly ground black pepper
4 eggs
4 soft flour tortilla wraps
Lime wedges, to serve

● **1** Preheat the oven to 220°C/425°F/Gas 7. Heat 1 tablespoon oil in a large frying pan over a high heat. Add the onion and cook for 2 minutes, stirring occasionally. Add the peppers and chilli flakes and cook for 5 minutes before adding the tomatoes and paprika. Cook until the tomatoes just start to break down. Stir in the beans and season well with salt and black pepper.

● **2** Using the back of a spoon, make 4 indents in the mixture, then crack an egg into each hollow and bake for 10–12 minutes until the eggs are cooked to your liking.

● **3** Lightly brush both sides of the tortilla wraps with olive oil, cut or tear into triangles and place on a large baking sheet – don't overlap them. Bake for 5 minutes, turning halfway through, until golden. Remove from the oven and leave to crisp on the hot tray. Serve with the baked eggs.

Calories per portion 510 Kcal ● Fat per portion 20g ● Serves 4

Serve with...

This spicy combination makes a great weekend brunch or supper dish.

✓ *Easy* Ⓝ *Contains Nuts* Ⓥ *Vegetarian*

Mediterranean Clafoutis

Preparation time 10 minutes ● Cooking time 40 minutes

Butter, to grease

1 teaspoon olive oil

3 courgettes, thinly sliced

1 aubergine, thinly sliced

Bunch fresh basil, chopped

6 eggs

6 tablespoons plain flour

400ml (14fl oz) milk

350ml (12fl oz) double cream

Salt and freshly ground black pepper

2 tablespoons pine nuts

● **1** Preheat the oven to 180°C/350°F/Gas 4. Grease a rectangular baking dish with butter. Heat the oil in a heavy-based pan and gently cook the vegetables for 15 minutes, stirring frequently to prevent burning. Add the basil and stir gently. Transfer to the baking dish.

● **2** In a mixing bowl beat the eggs and gradually add the flour, milk and cream, whisking continuously to form a smooth batter. Season with salt and pepper. Pour the batter onto the vegetables and bake for 25 minutes until set and golden. Sprinkle with pine nuts. Serve immediately.

Calories per portion 502 Kcal ● Fat per portion 43.5g ● Serves 6

Serve with...

Serve this tasty bake with a green salad or mixed steamed vegetables.

✓ *Easy* Ⓥ *Vegetarian*

Vegetable & Egg Pan-fry

Preparation time 15 minutes ● Cooking time 30 minutes

1 tablespoon olive oil

6 mixed red, yellow or orange peppers, deseeded and sliced into strips

Pinch brown sugar

225g bag baby spinach

Salt and freshly ground black pepper

4 eggs

● **1** Heat the oil in a large frying pan. Add the peppers and cook for 15–20 minutes over a low heat until beginning to soften. Sprinkle with the sugar and stir. Add the spinach, a little at a time, stirring until wilted. Season with salt and freshly ground black pepper.

● **2** Preheat the grill to high. Using a spoon, make four shallow dents in the mixture and crack an egg into each one. Turn up the heat and cook for 2–3 minutes, then place the frying pan under the grill and cook until the eggs are cooked to your liking.

Calories per portion 180 Kcal ● Fat per portion 8g ● Serves 4

Serve with...

Serve this simple dish with crusty bread and a green salad.

Make it spicy...

Add a pinch of dried chilli flakes with the sugar in step 1 for a spicy kick.

Quick ✓ *Easy* *Vegetarian*

Eggs Florentine

Preparation time 5 minutes ● Cooking time 20 minutes

4 tomatoes

Salt and freshly ground black pepper

250g bag baby spinach leaves

4 eggs

Pinch of paprika or cayenne pepper

● **1** Make a cross on the base of each tomato, place in a bowl and cover with boiling water. Count to ten, then remove and place in cold water. Drain and peel away the skins. Cut in half and remove the seeds, then chop the flesh, sprinkle with a little salt and set aside.

● **2** Place the spinach in a pan, sprinkle with a little water and cook for a few minutes until wilted. Drain with a slotted spoon and squeeze away any excess water. Mix with the tomatoes. Season and divide between 4 plates.

● **3** Crack one egg at a time into the centre of a pan of boiling salted water. Reduce to a simmer and cook for 4 minutes. Carefully remove with a slotted spoon, place on a piece of kitchen paper to drain, then place on top of the spinach. Sprinkle with paprika or cayenne and serve.

Calories per portion 120 Kcal ● Fat per portion 7g ● Serves 4

Serve with...

Serve this elegant dish with buttered toast or English muffins.

✓ *Easy* Ⓥ *Vegetarian*

Mixed Vegetable Fritters

Preparation time 5 minutes ● Cooking time 30 minutes

Sunflower oil, to deep-fry

1 courgette, cut into strips

1 aubergine, cut into strips

2 peppers, deseeded and cut into strips

For the batter

150g (5oz) plain flour

Salt

1 teaspoon baking powder

Pinch cayenne pepper

1 tablespoon olive oil

1 large egg

● **1** To make the batter, place the flour in a bowl and make a well in the centre. Add ½ teaspoon salt, the baking powder, cayenne, olive oil and egg. Slowly whisk in 250ml (9fl oz) cold water to make a smooth batter.

● **2** Heat about 5cm (2in) oil in a shallow pan until hot enough so a small cube of bread dropped into the oil turns golden in about 40 seconds. (If using a deep-fat fryer, heat to 180°C.)

● **3** Dip the vegetables into the batter, a few at a time, then carefully lower into the oil and cook until golden, turning now and again. Leave to drain on kitchen paper and keep warm. Cook in batches so the pan doesn't get overcrowded.

Calories per portion 211 Kcal ● Fat per portion 11g ● Serves 6

Serve with...

Serve these crispy vegetables with a dip made from Greek yogurt with either mint sauce and crushed garlic, harissa, curry powder and mango chutney, or smooth or grainy mustard stirred in.

Why not try...

You can make the fritters in advance and reheat in a hot oven to recrisp.

Quick ✓✓ Extra Easy V Vegetarian

Baked Eggs with Spinach

Preparation time 15 minutes ● Cooking time 15 minutes

3 tomatoes, finely chopped

Salt and freshly ground black pepper

125g pack mozzarella, sliced

Handful fresh basil leaves, torn

Large handful baby spinach leaves, chopped

Pinch freshly grated nutmeg

4 eggs

● **1** Preheat the oven to 200°C/400°F/Gas 6. Divide the tomatoes between 4 ramekins or ovenproof dishes. Season with salt and pepper. Add a couple mozzarella slices to each dish then top with the basil, spinach and nutmeg.

● **2** Make a little well in each dish and crack an egg into it. Bake for about 10–15 minutes until the white is set and the yolk is still just runny. Serve.

Calories per portion 193 Kcal ● Fat per portion 13g ● Serves 4

Serve with...

Serve this simple comforting supper with some fresh crusty bread.

Make it spicy...

Add a pinch of dried chilli flakes to the spinach for a spicy kick.

✓ *Easy* Ⓥ *Vegetarian*

Paprika Potato Tortilla

Preparation time 20 minutes ● Cooking time 40 minutes

550g (1¼lb) new potatoes

3 tablespoons olive oil

2 onions, sliced

2 teaspoons smoked paprika

6 eggs

75g (3oz) Manchego or Cheddar, grated

Salt and freshly ground black pepper

● **1** Cook the potatoes in a pan of boiling water for 15 minutes until just tender. Drain, cool then slice thinly. Meanwhile, heat the oil in a large frying pan and cook the onions over a medium heat for 8–10 minutes until softened. Stir in the paprika and cook for 1 minute. Add the sliced potatoes and cook for a few minutes.

● **2** Preheat the grill to medium-high. Beat together the eggs and cheese and season with salt and pepper. Pour into the pan and cook over a medium heat for 10–15 minutes until just firming up. Grill for another 5–10 minutes until completely set and golden on top. Cut into wedges to serve.

Calories per portion 200 Kcal ● Fat per portion 12.5g ● Serves 8

Serve with...

This tasty tortilla can be served hot or cold with a mixed salad.

Why not try...

You can add other ingredients, such as sliced peppers, mushrooms, diced ham or crispy bacon bits.

✓ *Easy* Ⓝ *Contains Nuts* Ⓥ *Vegetarian*

Camembert Croquettes

Preparation time 15 minutes ● Cooking time 20 minutes

1 Camembert

50g (2oz) plain flour

Freshly ground black pepper

1 egg, beaten

150g (5oz) fresh breadcrumbs

Oil, for deep frying

For the grapes

Bunch white seedless grapes

50g (2oz) caster sugar

Handful chopped walnuts

● **1** Slice the grapes in half and place in a heavy-based pan with the sugar and enough water to cover the base of the pan. Cook over a low heat until the sugar has dissolved, stirring continuously.

● **2** Bring to the boil and simmer for 2–3 minutes. Pour into a dish and leave to cool. Sprinkle with the chopped walnuts. Cut the Camembert into 8 wedges. Place the flour and some black pepper in a plastic food bag.

● **3** Gently tip the cheese wedges into the bag and shake to cover completely with the flour mixture. Remove from the bag and dip into the beaten egg and then into the breadcrumbs until completely covered.

● **4** Heat the oil in a heavy-based pan and deep-fry the cheese wedges for 3–5 minutes until golden brown and crisp. Remove from the pan and drain on kitchen paper. Serve immediately with the grapes and walnuts.

Calories per portion 599 Kcal ● Fat per portion 33.5g ● Serves 4

Serve with...

This makes a tasty starter or lunch dish. Instead of the grapes, serve with spicy tomato relish or redcurrant jelly.

Why not try...

This dish also works well with Brie or firm goat's cheese.

Make it at the Weekend *Vegetarian*

Simple Cheese Soufflé

Preparation time 20 minutes ● Cooking time 30 minutes

25g (1oz) butter

Dried breadcrumbs, to dust

25g (1oz) plain flour

150ml (¼pt) milk

4 eggs, separated

175g (6oz) Gruyère, grated

1 tablespoon creamed horseradish

- **1** Preheat the oven to 200°C/400°F/Gas 6. Prepare a soufflé or ovenproof dish by rubbing a little butter around the edges and dusting with breadcrumbs.
- **2** Melt the remaining butter in a large pan, then add the flour and stir for a few minutes. Remove from the heat and gradually pour in the milk, stirring, until smooth. Return to the heat and continue stirring until the sauce starts to thicken, then remove from heat again.
- **3** Whisk the egg whites until soft peaks form and set aside. Whisk the egg yolks into the sauce and stir in the cheese and horseradish. Using a metal spoon, fold in the egg whites, a spoonful at a time, until combined.
- **4** Spoon into the dish and run a knife over the top to smooth. Place the dish on a baking tray, then bake for 30 minutes until risen and golden.

Calories per portion 360 Kcal ● Fat per portion 28g ● Serves 4

Serve with...

Serve this light, fluffy soufflé with a tomato and basil salad.

Why not try...

You can replace the horseradish with wholegrain or Dijon mustard if you prefer. Use any hard cheese, such as Cheddar, Emmental or Gouda.

Make it at the Weekend *Vegetarian*

Mozzarella Rice Balls

Preparation time 20 minutes ● Cooking time 45 minutes

1 tablespoon olive oil

1 onion, finely chopped

300g (11oz) risotto rice

600ml (1pt) hot vegetable stock

Salt and freshly ground black pepper

Handful fresh basil, finely torn

Handful fresh flat-leaf parsley, finely chopped

50g (2oz) Grana Padano, grated

2 eggs, lightly beaten

125g pack mozzarella, torn into chunks

75g (3oz) fresh breadcrumbs

Melted butter, for brushing

● **1** Heat the oil in a large saucepan, add the onion and cook until soft. Add the rice and stir well. Pour in a little stock, stirring, until absorbed. Continue adding the stock in this way until it is all absorbed and the rice is tender – this will take about 15 minutes. Season with salt and pepper, then leave to cool.

● **2** Preheat the oven to 200°C/400°F/Gas 6. Stir the herbs and Grana Padano into the risotto, then add the eggs and stir until the mixture binds together.

● **3** Scoop up a large handful of rice, then top with mozzarella. Top with some more rice and mould into a ball. Roll in breadcrumbs and place on an oiled baking sheet. Repeat to make 6 balls. Brush with melted butter and bake for 10–15 minutes until golden.

Calories per portion 387 Kcal ● Fat per portion 12g ● Makes 6

Serve with...

A simple rocket or watercress salad goes well with this hearty dish.

✓✓ *Extra Easy* 🌶 *Spicy* Ⓥ *Vegetarian*

Roasted Pumpkin with Brie

Preparation time 10 minutes ● Cooking time 25 minutes

1 small pumpkin

2 tablespoons olive oil

Salt

1 red chilli, finely diced

225g (8oz) Brie or Camembert, sliced

● **1** Preheat the oven to 200°C/400°F/Gas 6. Cut the pumpkin into 12 wedges and scoop out the seeds. Place the wedges in a roasting tray and drizzle with olive oil. Season with salt and sprinkle with the diced red chilli.

● **2** Roast for 20 minutes until the pumpkin is tender. Top each wedge with cheese and bake for 2–5 minutes until the cheese has melted. Serve.

Calories per portion 175 Kcal ● Fat per portion 14g ● Serves 6

Serve with...

Serve this tasty dish with a spinach, potato, radish and red onion salad.

Why not try...

This also works with butternut squash instead of pumpkin.

Extra Easy (V) *Vegetarian*

Two Cheese Fondue

Preparation time 5 minutes ● Cooking time 10 minutes

1 onion, halved and sliced
1 tablespoon dry white wine
2 garlic cloves, finely chopped
2 teaspoons mango chutney
Handful fresh flat-leaf parsley, chopped
225g (8oz) mix of Cheddar and Gruyère, grated

● **1** Place the onions in a pan with a little water and cook gently until the water has evaporated and the onions are soft. Increase the heat and stir in the wine, garlic, chutney and parsley. Add the cheese and cook over a low heat, stirring, until melted and smooth.

Calories per portion 253 Kcal ● Fat per portion 19.3g ● Serves 4

Serve with...

Serve this indulgent dish with slices of baked or toasted baguette to dip in. Alternatively, serve breadsticks, carrot and celery sticks as dippers.

✓ *Easy* Ⓥ *Vegetarian*

Peppers with Goat's Cheese

Preparation time 10 minutes ● Cooking time 15 minutes

175g (6oz) ready-made couscous salad
100g (3½oz) goat's cheese
1 tablespoon chopped fresh thyme
Salt and freshly ground black pepper
2 tablespoons olive oil
1 bag baby sweet peppers, halved lengthways and deseeded

● **1** Preheat the oven to 180°C/350°F/Gas 4. Mix the couscous salad with the goat's cheese and thyme. Season and drizzle with olive oil.

● **2** Spoon the mixture into the halved peppers. Place on an oiled baking tray and roast for 15 minutes until hot and the peppers are tender.

Calories per portion 58 Kcal ● Fat per portion 3.8g ● Makes 12

Serve with...

This easy colourful dish makes a great party dish or light lunch.

Make it at the Weekend · *Vegetarian*

Cheese & Herb Galette

Preparation time 15 minutes plus cooling ● Cooking time 1 hour

Large pinch saffron strands
1.2 ltr (2pts) hot vegetable stock
50g (2oz) butter
1 onion, finely chopped
3 garlic cloves, crushed
350g (12oz) risotto rice
125ml (4fl oz) dry white wine
4 tablespoons chopped mixed fresh herbs, such as basil, chives, parsley and tarragon
25g (1oz) grated Parmesan
2 large eggs, beaten
225g (8oz) Taleggio, rind removed and cubed
Salt and freshly ground black pepper
Oil, for shallow frying

● **1** Add the saffron strands to the hot stock and leave to infuse for 10 minutes. Melt the butter in a frying pan, add the onion and garlic and fry for 10 minutes until soft and golden. Add the rice and stir for 1 minute until all the grains are glossy.

● **2** Add the wine and boil rapidly until almost all the liquid has evaporated. Heat the stock and keep at a low simmer. Add 1 ladleful of stock to the rice and simmer gently, stirring, until absorbed. Continue to add stock and stir for 20–25 minutes until all the stock is used and the rice is tender.

● **3** Remove the risotto from the heat, then stir in the herbs and Parmesan. Cover the surface with greaseproof paper and leave to cool.

● **4** Preheat the oven to 170°C/325°F/Gas 3. Stir the eggs into the risotto, then divide the mixture in half. Brush a 23cm (9in) ovenproof pan with a little oil. Spoon half the risotto into the pan and spread evenly to the edges with a palette knife. Sprinkle the diced Taleggio on top, then spread the rest of the risotto over the top. Bake for 15–20 minutes until piping hot.

● **5** Preheat the grill to high. Place the pan under the grill until the top is golden. Leave in the pan to cool for 10 minutes before serving.

Calories per portion 341 Kcal ● Fat per portion 16.4g ● Serves 8

Serve with...

Serve this new-look risotto with a simple green salad.

✓ *Easy* Ⓥ *Vegetarian*

Asparagus & Parmesan Flan

Preparation time 15 minutes ● Cooking time 1 hour

Butter, to grease

500g (18oz) fine asparagus spears

Salt and freshly ground black pepper

250ml (9fl oz) double cream

3 eggs

50g (2oz) Parmesan, grated

Small bunch fresh chives, chopped

● **1** Preheat the oven to 150°C/300°F/Gas 2. Liberally butter 6 ramekin dishes. Cook the asparagus in a pan of boiling salted water for 5–8 minutes until just tender. Drain on kitchen paper, then chop into small pieces. Transfer to a bowl and add the cream, eggs and Parmesan. Season and mix well.

● **2** Pour the mixture into the ramekins. Place in a large baking tin and pour in enough hot water to come halfway up the sides of the dishes.

● **3** Bake for 40–50 minutes until firm. Check after 25 minutes and cover with foil if they are beginning to dry out too much. Leave in the roasting tin to cool slightly. Decorate with chopped chives and a twist of black pepper.

Calories per portion 332 Kcal ● Fat per portion 31.5g ● Serves 6

Serve with...

Serve these delicate bakes warm or cold with mixed green salad leaves.

Make it at the Weekend ❄ *Freeze it* Ⓥ *Vegetarian*

Cheese, Onion & Potato Pies

Preparation time 20 minutes plus chilling ● Cooking time 1 hour

500g (18oz) shortcrust pastry

1 tablespoon olive oil

1 onion, finely chopped

1 medium potato, grated

284ml carton single cream

2 large eggs, plus 1 beaten egg, to glaze

1 teaspoon smooth mustard

75g (3oz) Gruyère, grated

Salt and freshly ground black pepper

● **1** Preheat the oven to 200°C/400°F/Gas 6. Roll out two-thirds of the pastry on a floured surface and use to line 2 x 11.5cm (4½in) loose-based deep pork pie tins, allowing the pastry to overlap the sides. Chill for 20 minutes. Line with greaseproof paper and fill with baking beans. Bake for 15 minutes. Remove the paper and beans, and bake for 5 minutes until cooked.

● **2** Heat the oil in a frying pan and cook the onion and potato, stirring frequently to keep them broken up. Whisk together the cream, eggs, mustard and cheese in a large measuring jug and season. Add the onion and potatoes and combine. Pour into the pastry cases.

● **3** Roll out the remaining pastry to make 2 lids. Brush the edge of the pastry with beaten egg and press the lids on top of the pies. Brush with egg and bake for 30 minutes until golden and cooked through. To test if the pie is cooked, insert a cocktail stick into the top of pie – if it comes out clean, it is ready. Leave for 5 minutes before serving.

Calories per portion 599 Kcal ● Fat per portion 44.9g ● Serves 6

Serve with...

Serve these tasty pies warm with a dollop of chutney and some salad.

Why not try...

If you don't have the pork pie tins, use a 20.5cm (8in) loose-based sandwich tin. You can freeze the pies before baking then defrost and bake for 30–45 minutes until piping hot.

Super Quick ✓✓ Extra Easy Spicy

Warm Goat's Cheese & Chilli

Preparation time 10 minutes ● Cooking time 5 minutes

2 x 100g round goat's cheeses, halved
1 red chilli, deseeded and finely chopped
2 tablespoons fresh flat-leaf parsley, roughly chopped
Good drizzle extra-virgin olive oil
Juice of ½ lemon, plus extra wedges for serving

● **1** Preheat the grill to high. Place the cheeses on a baking tray and grill until warmed through and starting to melt. Transfer to a plate and scatter over the chopped chilli and parsley. Drizzle with olive oil and lemon juice, and serve with extra lemon wedges.

Calories per portion 210 Kcal ● Fat per portion 18g ● Serves 4

Serve with...

This simple but sensational combination just needs some crusty fresh bread on the side.

Why not try...

This dressing also works well with good-quality mozzarella. Thickly slice and top with the chilli, parsley, oil and lemon juice – there's no need to cook.

Make it at the Weekend *Freeze it*

Macaroni Cheese

Preparation time 15 minutes ● Cooking time 25 minutes

25g (1oz) butter

1 tablespoon olive oil

2 onions, finely chopped

225g (8oz) ham, chopped

275g (10oz) macaroni, cooked

For the sauce

75g (3oz) butter

75g (3oz) plain flour

850ml (1½pts) milk

200g (7oz) Gruyère, grated

½ teaspoon English mustard

Salt and freshly ground black pepper

- **Step 1** For the sauce, melt the butter in a pan, then stir in the flour. Cook over a medium heat for a few minutes, stirring, to make smooth paste.
- **Step 2** Add a little of the milk to the pan, stirring, until smooth. Repeat until all the milk has been added. Cook, stirring, until boiling and thickened.
- **Step 3** Stir in 150g (5oz) grated cheese, the mustard and seasoning and cook, stirring, until the cheese melts. Set aside.
- **4** Heat the butter and oil in a pan and fry the onions for 3–4 minutes until soft but not browned.
- **5** Preheat the grill to high. Mix together the onions, ham, macaroni and sauce and heat through. Spoon into a flameproof dish. Top with the remaining cheese. Grill until the cheese is melted and golden.

Calories per portion 464 Kcal ● Fat per portion 29.9g ● Serves 6

Step 1 *Melt the butter in a saucepan and add the flour. Stir over the heat to make a smooth paste (a 'roux').*

Step 2 *Add a little milk to the pan and stir until combined and smooth. Add the remaining milk in the same way.*

Step 3 *Stir the grated cheese into the sauce along with the mustard and seasoning. Stir until melted.*

✓ *Easy* Ⓥ *Vegetarian*

Baked Potatoes with Feta

Preparation time 10 minutes ● Cooking time 35 minutes

3 tablespoons olive oil

1.1kg (2½lb) new potatoes, halved

4 sprigs fresh rosemary

2 garlic cloves, chopped

Salt and freshly ground black pepper

6 vine tomatoes, cut into chunks

2 tablespoons black olives

200g pack feta cheese, crumbled

● **1** Preheat the oven to 200°C/400°F/Gas 6. Place the oil in a roasting tin and heat in the oven until hot. Add the potatoes, rosemary and garlic and season with salt and pepper. Stir to coat in the oil.

● **2** Roast for 20 minutes. Add the tomatoes, olives and feta and bake for a further 10 minutes until the potatoes are tender. Serve immediately.

Calories per portion 425 Kcal ● Fat per portion 20g ● Serves 4

Serve with...

Serve as a vegetarian meal or as a side dish with fish or roast lamb.

✓ *Easy*

Cheesy Stuffed Chicken

Preparation time 15 minutes ● Cooking time 40 minutes

150g tub soft goat's cheese

Bunch fresh thyme leaves, chopped

200g can pitted green olives, half chopped

Salt and freshly ground black pepper

4 boneless chicken breasts or thighs, skin on

450g (1lb) baby new potatoes, halved

1½ tablespoons olive oil

● **1** Preheat the oven to 200°C/400°F/Gas 6. Mix the goat's cheese in a small bowl with 2 tablespoons thyme leaves, the chopped olives and plenty of salt and black pepper. Peel back part of the chicken skin to make an opening and stuff the cheese mixture under the skin.

● **2** Place the chicken in a roasting dish. Add the potatoes to the dish and drizzle with olive oil until well coated. Season with salt and black pepper and a handful of thyme. Roast for 35–40 minutes until the chicken is golden, crispy and cooked. Serve with the remaining olives scattered over.

Calories per portion 560 Kcal ● Fat per portion 30g ● Serves 4

Serve with...

This all-in-one dish is great served with focaccia bread and rocket salad.

✓ *Easy* Ⓥ *Vegetarian*

Chargrilled Veg & Halloumi

Preparation time 15 minutes ● Cooking time 25 minutes

2 small aubergines, cut lengthways into 8 wedges
4 courgettes, quartered lengthways
3 tablespoons olive oil
Zest of 1 orange and juice of ½
1 teaspoon clear honey
2 teaspoons cider vinegar
50g (2oz) pitted black olives, sliced
Bunch fresh flat-leaf parsley, chopped
Freshly ground black pepper
200g pack half-fat halloumi, sliced into 8

● **1** Brush each wedge of aubergine and courgette with a little of the olive oil. Preheat a ridged griddle pan until very hot and add a layer of vegetables. Cook on each side until nicely charred, then transfer to a large plate. Repeat until all the vegetables are cooked.

● **2** Meanwhile, whisk together the remaining olive oil, orange zest and juice, honey, vinegar, olives and most of the parsley. Season with black pepper. Drizzle a little dressing over each batch of hot grilled vegetables.

● **3** Just before serving, cook the halloumi on the griddle for a few minutes on each side. Scatter the vegetables with the remaining parsley, top with halloumi and drizzle with the remaining dressing.

Calories per portion 271 Kcal ● Fat per portion 21g ● Serves 4

Serve with…

Serve this dish with a scattering of toasted pine nuts and some warm flatbreads.

✓ *Easy* Ⓥ *Vegetarian*

Stuffed Peppers with Feta

Preparation time 15 minutes ● Cooking time 30 minutes

2 red peppers

2 tomatoes, cut into quarters

1 garlic clove, finely chopped

2 teaspoons capers

2 tablespoons chopped fresh basil

2 teaspoons olive oil

2 teaspoons balsamic vinegar

50g (2oz) feta

● **1** Preheat the oven to 180°C/350°F/Gas 4. Cut the red peppers in half, leaving the stalk intact, and remove the seeds and pith. Fill with the tomato quarters then divide the garlic, capers and basil between them, tucking into and under the tomatoes. Place in an ovenproof dish.

● **2** Pour over the oil and balsamic vinegar and bake for 30 minutes until the peppers are soft, juicy and wrinkled around the edges. Remove from the oven and crumble over the feta cheese.

Calories per portion 165 Kcal ● Fat per portion 9.9g ● Serves 2

Serve with...

Serve the peppers with slices of ciabatta and a simple green salad.

Why not try...

Replace the feta with goat's cheese or diced mozzarella.

Extra Easy ● *Vegetarian*

Roasted Pepper Melt

Preparation time 15 minutes ● Cooking time 35 minutes

4 red peppers, deseeded and roughly chopped

4 orange peppers, deseeded and roughly chopped

2 x 150g packs sweet baby orange peppers, quartered

2 fennel bulbs, roughly chopped

Salt and freshly ground black pepper

Olive oil, to drizzle

Fresh thyme stalks

1 whole Camembert

- **1** Preheat the oven to 200°C/400°F/Gas 6. Place the peppers and fennel in a large roasting tin or oven proof dish. Season with salt and black pepper and drizzle with olive oil. Throw in a few thyme stalks and toss together.

- **2** Roast for 20 minutes until the peppers are lightly charred and the fennel is almost cooked. Score the Camembert into 8, then place on top of the vegetables and cook for 10–15 minutes until the Camembert begins to melt over the vegetables.

Calories per portion 194 Kcal ● Fat per portion 13.2g ● Serves 8

Serve with...

Serve this simple vegetarian dish with crusty baguette or sourdough bread.

✓ *Easy* Ⓥ *Vegetarian*

Cheese & Rosemary Pots

Preparation time 15 minutes ● Cooking time 25 minutes

1 teaspoon melted butter

4 tablespoons self-raising flour, plus extra, to dust

75g (3oz) very strong Cheddar, chopped into small cubes

75g (3oz) red Leicester, chopped into small cubes

125g (4oz) fresh white breadcrumbs

2 large shallots, finely chopped

2 teaspoons finely chopped fresh rosemary, plus 4 small sprigs

½ bunch fresh parsley, roughly chopped

½ teaspoon English mustard powder

Salt and freshly ground black pepper

3 eggs, beaten

6 tablespoons milk

● **1** Preheat the oven to 190°C/375°F/Gas 5. Brush 4 x 150ml (¼pt) ramekins with the melted butter, then dust with a little flour to coat thoroughly. Place the cheeses, breadcrumbs, shallots, chopped rosemary, parsley, mustard and flour in a bowl. Season well and stir to combine.

● **2** Add the eggs and milk and mix until well combined. Spoon the mixture into the dishes, filling to the top. Push a rosemary sprig on top of each, then place on a baking tray and bake for 25 minutes until golden and springy. Turn out of the dishes and serve.

Calories per portion 430 Kcal ● Fat per portion 21g ● Serves 4

Serve with...

Serve these tasty cheese bakes with a spicy mango or pear chutney.

Quick *Extra Easy* *Vegetarian*

Baked Goat's Cheese Parcels

Preparation time 5 minutes ● Cooking time 20 minutes

6 firm goat's cheeses, at room temperature
6 tablespoons olive oil, plus a little extra for drizzling
6 sprigs fresh thyme

1 Preheat the oven to 190°C/375°F/Gas 5 or heat a barbecue until hot. Place each cheese in a 10cm (4in) foil square and pull up the sides. Drizzle 1 tablespoon oil over each cheese and top with sprigs of thyme. Close the foil, scrunching to seal, and cook for 15–20 minutes until the cheese begins to melt. Drizzle with extra oil to serve.

Calories per portion 200 Kcal ● Fat per portion 23g ● Serves 6

Serve with...

Serve the baked cheese on toasted bread spread with roasted garlic or garlic butter.

Why not try...

Add a drizzle of clear honey to the cheeses with the oil.

◕ *Make it at the Weekend* Ⓥ *Vegetarian*

Four Cheese Focaccia

Preparation time 15 minutes plus rising ● Cooking time 20 minutes

500g pack ciabatta bread mix

2 tablespoons olive oil, plus extra to drizzle

Flour, for dusting

400g (14oz) four mixed cheeses, such as soft pressed goat's cheese, Lancashire, Wensleydale, Stilton or Dovedale blue, crumbled or grated

Few sprigs fresh rosemary

● **1** Preheat the oven to 220°C/425°F/Gas 7. Place the bread mix in a food processor with 350ml (12fl oz) warm water. Using a dough paddle, mix together for 5 minutes to form a dough. Add the oil and continue to mix for a further 5–8 minutes.

● **2** With floured hands, remove the dough and knead gently for a couple of minutes. Place in a large bowl, cover with cling film and leave to rise in a warm place for 20 minutes until doubled in size.

● **3** Divide the dough in half. Knead for a few minutes then roll out each to a large circle. Transfer to lightly oiled baking sheets and scatter a different cheese into each quarter. Scatter with some rosemary leaves, then bake for 15–20 minutes until golden and risen. Serve warm.

Calories per portion 330 Kcal ● Fat per portion 5g ● Serves 8

Serve with...

This tasty bread makes a great party nibble or starter. Or serve as an accompaniment to a pasta dish.

Quick ✓ Easy

Mushroom & Brie Salad

Preparation time 5 minutes ● Cooking time 12 minutes

- 130g pack pancetta or streaky bacon, diced
- 4 tablespoons olive oil
- 2 tablespoons balsamic vinegar
- 50g (2oz) black olives, pitted and chopped
- 4 large brown cap mushrooms
- 150g (5oz) Brie, sliced
- 4 sprigs fresh thyme
- Freshly ground black pepper
- 250g bag baby spinach

● **1** Preheat the grill to high. For the dressing, fry the pancetta or bacon until crispy, then remove from the pan and drain on kitchen paper. In a bowl, mix together the olive oil, balsamic vinegar, pancetta and olives. Set aside.

● **2** Grill the mushrooms on a grill rack for 5 minutes until tender. Top with the Brie, thyme and a grinding of black pepper. Grill for a further 2 minutes until the cheese has melted. To serve, divide the spinach between 4 plates, drizzle over the dressing and place the mushrooms on top.

Calories per portion 350 Kcal ● Fat per portion 30.6g ● Serves 4

Serve with...

A basket of crusty bread is all you need to complete this simple rustic meal.

Why not try...

For extra flavour, brush the mushrooms with garlic butter before grilling.

● *Make it at the Weekend* Ⓥ *Vegetarian*

Hot & Sweet Quiche Royale

Preparation time 30 minutes plus resting ● Cooking time 1 hour 5 minutes

375g pack shortcrust pastry

Salt and freshly ground black pepper

1 red and 1 yellow pepper, deseeded and quartered

40g (1½oz) butter

1½ teaspoons vegetable oil

2 large onions, thinly sliced

2 eggs, plus 1 egg yolk

150ml (¼pt) double cream

125g (4oz) Gruyère or Cheddar, grated

- **1** Preheat the oven to 220°C/425°F/Gas 7. Roll out the pastry on a floured surface and top with a generous grinding of black pepper. Roll in to the pastry then use to line a 20.5cm (8in) round flan tin. Line with greaseproof paper and baking beans and bake for 15 minutes. Remove the beans and paper and bake for a further 5 minutes until pale golden.

- **2** Preheat the grill to high. Grill the peppers, skin-side up, until the skins blister. Cool slightly, then peel off the skins and cut the peppers into strips.

- **3** Reduce the oven to 160°C/325°F/Gas 3. Melt half the butter with 1 tablespoon oil in a frying pan. Cook the onions until soft and transparent. Leave to cool. Melt the rest of the butter and oil together and leave to cool.

- **4** Beat together the eggs and egg yolk, then add the cream and stir in the cheese and cooled butter mixture. Carefully stir in the pepper strips. Season.

- **5** Pour into the pastry case and bake for 35–45 minutes until the flan is just set – it should be just firm to the touch and lightly browned. Leave to rest for 20–30 minutes before serving.

Calories per portion 630 Kcal ● Fat per portion 50.3g ● Serves 6

Serve with...

A tomato salad dressed with olive oil, salt and black pepper goes really well with the warm quiche.

✓ *Easy* ❄ *Freeze it* 🌶 *Spicy*

Spicy Coconut Pancakes

Preparation time 10 minutes ● Cooking time 30 minutes

125g (4oz) plain flour
400ml can coconut milk
1 egg
1 teaspoon ground coriander
2 teaspoons cumin seeds
Salt and freshly ground black pepper
Vegetable oil, for frying
400g can chopped tomatoes with chilli
5cm (2in) piece fresh ginger, grated
500g (18oz) cooked peeled prawns
2 tablespoons chopped fresh coriander

● **1** Mix together the flour, coconut milk, egg, coriander and cumin in a bowl or food processor and season. Heat a little oil in a frying pan and pour in a ladleful of the batter. Cook for 1 minute on each side until lightly browned. Remove from the pan and keep warm. Repeat with the remaining mixture.

● **2** Place the tomatoes and ginger in a saucepan and bring to the boil. Turn down the heat and simmer for 10–15 minutes until thickened. Add the prawns and cook for 1 minute until heated through. Stir in the coriander and serve with the warm pancakes.

Calories per portion 325 Kcal ● Fat per portion 8g ● Serves 4

Why not try...

The pancakes and sauce can be made in advance and frozen. Layer the pancakes between sheets of greaseproof paper and wrap well in foil or freezer film. To serve, heat from frozen in a hot oven. Freeze the sauce without the prawns and coriander. Reheat in a pan then add the remaining ingredients.

Super Quick ✓✓ Extra Easy V Vegetarian

Melon & Feta Salad

Preparation time 15 minutes ● Cooking time none

4 tablespoons extra-virgin olive oil

2 tablespoons white wine vinegar

1 teaspoon caster sugar

200g pack feta cheese, cubed

½ watermelon, roughly sliced

½ Charantais melon, deseeded and roughly sliced

Handful fresh mint leaves, torn

Freshly ground black pepper

● **1** Place the oil, vinegar and sugar in a bowl and whisk until the sugar dissolves. Add the feta and toss together until the cheese is well coated.

● **2** In another bowl, mix together both types of melon and the dressed cheese. Scatter with mint, then toss to combine. Season with black pepper.

Calories per portion 321 Kcal ● Fat per portion 22g ● Serves 4

Serve with...

This cool, refreshing salad is perfect served with some crusty bread.

✓ *Easy* Ⓥ *Vegetarian*

Summer Fruit Pavlova

Preparation time 15 minutes plus cooling ● Cooking time 1 hour 30 minutes

6 egg whites

350g (12oz) golden caster sugar

1 teaspoon white wine vinegar

2 teaspoons cornflour

For the topping

284ml tub double cream, lightly whipped

Mixed summer fruits, such as strawberries, raspberries, blueberries and blackberries

Icing sugar, to dust

- **1** Preheat the oven to 180°C/350°F/Gas 4. Line a baking sheet with baking paper, place a dinner plate on top, draw around it and cut out a circle.

- **2** In a large mixing bowl, whisk the egg whites until stiff peaks form. Add the sugar, 1 tablespoon at a time, whisking after each addition until really stiff and glossy. Using a metal spoon, fold in the vinegar and cornflour.

- **3** Using a spatula, spoon the meringue and spread it on the circle of paper. Then, using a spoon, make a hollow in the centre for the fruit to sit in. Bake for 5 minutes, then turn the oven down to 130°C/250F/Gas ½ for 1–1½ hours. Turn off the oven and leave the meringue to cool completely inside.

- **4** Slide the meringue onto a plate and peel away the baking paper. Fill with cream and top with fruit. Dust with icing sugar just before serving.

Calories per portion 300 Kcal ● Fat per portion 15g ● Serves 10

Serve with...

Instead of cream, you could fill the pavlova with Greek yogurt, crème fraîche or even ice-cream.

◐ *Make it at the Weekend* Ⓝ *Contains Nuts* Ⓥ *Vegetarian*

Baked Egg Custard Tartlets

Preparation time 30 minutes plus cooling ● Cooking time 25 minutes

500ml (18fl oz) milk

1 vanilla pod

375g pack shortcrust pastry

3 eggs

125g (4oz) caster sugar

50g (2oz) plain or cornflour

6 teaspoons apricot jam

Handful toasted pine nuts

● **1** Pour the milk into a heavy-based saucepan. Split the vanilla pod, scrape the seeds into the milk and add the split pod. Bring the milk to the boil then set aside and leave to infuse.

● **2** Meanwhile, roll out the pastry and use to line 6 individual flan dishes or tart tins. Prick the bases with a fork and chill in the fridge for 20 minutes. Preheat the oven to 180°C/350°F/Gas 4.

● **3** In a bowl, beat together the eggs and caster sugar until pale and glossy, then stir in the flour. Strain the infused milk into the egg mixture, whisking continuously, until smooth and combined.

● **4** Pour the mixture into the pastry cases. Bake for 20 minutes until lightly browned and just set. Turn off the oven and leave the flans inside to cool.

● **5** When completely cold remove the tarts from the tins, take a small spoonful of egg custard from the centre of each flan and add a spoonful of apricot jam and a sprinkling of pine nuts.

Calories per portion 519 Kcal ● Fat per portion 27.5g ● Serves 6

Serve with...

These tarts are perfect as a pudding with whipped cream, or as a sweet treat with a cup of tea or coffee.

✓ *Easy* Ⓥ *Vegetarian*

American Cheesecake

Preparation time 20 minutes plus cooling ● Cooking time 55 minutes

25cm (10in) sponge flan case

Blueberries, to serve

Icing sugar, to dust

For the cheesecake

225g (8oz) caster sugar

3 tablespoons cornflour

700g (1½lb) full-fat cream cheese

2 eggs

1 vanilla pod, seeds scraped out

300ml (½pt) whipping cream

● **Step 1** Preheat the oven to 180°C/350°F/Gas 4. Using a 23cm (9in) cake tin as a template, cut away the rim of the flan case to fit. Trim horizontally to make a 1cm (½in) slice. Place in the base of the tin.

● **Step 2** Mix together the sugar and cornflour in a bowl then beat in the cheese until well mixed and smooth. Beat in the eggs and vanilla seeds.

● **3** Slowly pour the cream onto the cheesecake mixture, beating constantly to give a thick, creamy consistency.

● **Step 4** Pour the mixture over the sponge base in the tin. Set on the centre shelf of the oven and place a baking tray part-filled with warm water on the shelf below. Bake for 50–55 minutes until golden and just set.

● **5** Turn off the oven and leave the cheesecake inside for an extra 15 minutes. Remove from the oven and allow to cool completely. Serve decorated with fresh blueberries and dusted with icing sugar.

Calories per portion 761 Kcal ● Fat per portion 60.1g ● Serves 8

Step 1 *Using the base of the cake tin as a guide, trim off the rim of the sponge flan case so it will fit neatly in the tin.*

Step 2 *Beat the eggs and vanilla seeds into the cheese mixture. (You can mix in a food processor if you like.)*

Step 4 *Pour the cheese mixture onto the sponge cake base. Bake until golden and just set in the centre.*

● *Make it at the Weekend* Ⓝ *Contains Nuts*

Lemon & Lime Soufflé

Preparation time 1 hour plus chilling ● Cooking time 5 minutes

Oil, to grease

2 teaspoons powdered gelatine

4 large eggs, separated

125g (4oz) caster sugar

Zest and juice of 2 lemons (you need 125ml/4fl oz juice – top up with lime juice if needed)

300ml (½pt) double cream

Zest of 1 lime

25g (1oz) pistachio nuts, chopped

- **Step 1** Wrap a double strip of greaseproof paper around a 1.1 ltr (2pt) soufflé dish so it stands 5cm (2in) above the rim. Lightly oil the paper above the rim and secure with string. Sprinkle the gelatine over 3 tablespoons water in a bowl. Stand for 10 minutes to soften.

- **2** In a bowl, whisk the egg yolks and sugar for about 2 minutes until pale and beginning to thicken. Add the lemon juice and whisk for 2–3 minutes. Whip the cream until just holding its shape, then cover and chill.

- **3** Place the gelatine bowl over a pan of simmering water until dissolved. Pour into the creamy egg mixture, stirring continuously.

- **Step 4** Stand the bowl in a large bowl of ice-cold water. Stir constantly for 5–10 minutes until beginning to thicken. Remove from the water and fold in the cream, and the lemon and lime zests.

- **Step 5** Whisk the egg whites to stiff peaks. Gently fold into the lemon mix. Pour into the dish, tap gently to level and chill for 2–3 hours until set. Remove the paper. Decorate with nuts, pressing gently around the edge.

Calories per portion 380 Kcal ● Fat per portion 30g ● Serves 6

Step 1 *Wrap a double thickness of greaseproof paper around the dish, standing 5cm (2in) above the rim.*

Step 4 *Stand the bowl in a large bowl of ice-cold water and stir constantly until starting to thicken.*

Step 5 *Gently fold the whisked egg whites into the lemon mixture using a metal spoon until just combined.*

Make it at the Weekend · *Vegetarian*

Raspberry Meringue Roulade

Preparation time 30 minutes plus cooling ● Cooking time 1 hour

Oil, to grease
5 large egg whites
150g (5oz) caster sugar
2 teaspoons cornflour
1 teaspoon vanilla essence
1 teaspoon white wine vinegar
Icing or caster sugar, to dust
Raspberry coulis, to serve

For the filling
284ml carton double cream
1 teaspoon vanilla essence
50g (2oz) icing sugar
250g (9oz) raspberries

- **1** Preheat the oven to 150°C/300°F/Gas 2. Line a 33 x 28cm (13 x 11in) Swiss roll tin with oiled baking paper, leaving a 5cm (2in) overhang.

- **2** Whisk the egg whites in a large clean bowl until stiff peaks form. Gradually whisk in the caster sugar until the mixture is stiff and glossy.

- **Step 3** Gently fold in the cornflour, vanilla essence and vinegar. Scoop the meringue onto the lined tray, spreading it evenly right to the edges.

- **Step 4** Bake for 1 hour until pale golden with a light crust, then cool in the tin. Sprinkle a sheet of greaseproof paper with icing or caster sugar and turn out the meringue onto it. Peel off the lining paper.

- **Step 5** Whip the cream to soft peaks and fold in the vanilla and icing sugar. Spread over the meringue, leaving a 2.5cm (1in) border around the edge. Scatter the raspberries evenly over the cream and carefully roll up. Serve with more raspberries and a raspberry coulis.

Calories per portion 414 Kcal ● Fat per portion 26.4g ● Serves 6

Step 3 *Gently fold the cornflour, vanilla and vinegar into the egg whites with a spatula or metal spoon.*

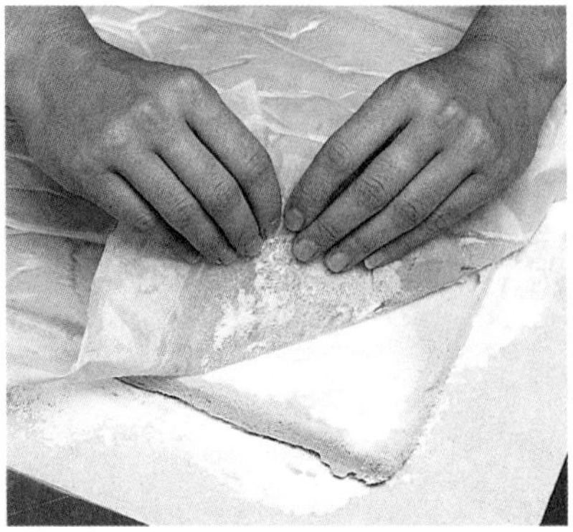

Step 4 *Turn out the meringue onto a sheet of greaseproof paper dusted with sugar then peel off the baking paper.*

Step 5 *Carefully roll the meringue around the filling using the paper to help you – don't worry if it cracks a bit.*

Weights, measures & temperatures

TEMPERATURE

°C	°F	Gas	°C	°F	Gas
110	225	¼	190	375	5
120/130	250	½	200	400	6
140	275	1	220	425	7
150	300	2	230	450	8
160/170	325	3	240	475	9
180	350	4			

LIQUIDS

Metric	Imperial	Metric	Imperial
5ml	1 tsp	200ml	7fl oz
15ml	1 tbsp	250ml	9fl oz
25ml	1fl oz	300ml	½ pint
50ml	2fl oz	500ml	18fl oz
100ml	3½fl oz	600ml	1 pint
125ml	4fl oz	900ml	1½ pints
150ml	5fl oz/¼ pint	1 litre	1¾ pints
175ml	6fl oz		

ABOUT THE RECIPES

Recipes that are suitable for freezing are indicated at the top of the recipe. For further guidance, see below and consult your freezer manufacturer's guidelines.

MEASURES

Metric	Imperial	Metric	Imperial
5mm	¼in	10cm	4in
1cm	½in	15cm	6in
2cm	¾in	18cm	7in
2.5cm	1in	20.5cm	8in
3cm	1¼in	23cm	9in
4cm	1½in	25.5cm	10in
5cm	2in	28cm	11in
7.5cm	3in	30.5cm	12in

WEIGHTS

Metric	Imperial	Metric	Imperial
15g	½oz	275g	10oz
25g	1oz	300g	11oz
40g	1½oz	350g	12oz
50g	2oz	375g	13oz
75g	3oz	400g	14oz
100g	3½oz	425g	15oz
125g	4oz	450g	1lb
150g	5oz	550g	1¼lb
175g	6oz	700g	1½lb
200g	7oz	900g	2lb
225g	8oz	1.1kg	2½lb
250g	9oz		

Food safety & hygiene

- Always wash your hands before handling any food.
- Always wash fruit and vegetables before using them.
- Ensure your work surfaces and chopping boards are clean. Keep a separate chopping board for preparing raw meat.
- Cool leftover food as quickly as possible, ideally within one to two hours, and then store covered in the fridge.
- Leftover rice must be stored covered and for no longer than one day.
- Do not buy cracked eggs.
- If you are reheating food, make sure you heat all the way through and until it is piping hot. Do not reheat food more than once. Do not keep leftovers for longer than two days.
- Once thawed, do not refreeze raw food unless you have cooked it first.
- Read and follow the use-by dates on packaging and jars.
- Children, pregnant women or the elderly should not eat recipes that contain raw eggs.
- Ensure that your fridge is 5°C or less and the deep freeze is at least -20°C.
- Change and wash tea towels, towels, dishcloths, aprons and oven gloves often. Keep your pets away from surfaces and tables.
- Organise your fridge so that meat is kept separately and on the bottom shelf. Keep dairy produce together and fruit, vegetables and salad ingredients in the salad compartment.
- Store raw foods separately from cooked foods to avoid contamination.
- After shopping, put all food for the refrigerator and freezer into their allotted places as soon as possible.